A Place to Talk *in*
Pre-schools

'It's true, sometimes we just can't see the wood for the trees. Not only does Elizabeth Jarman provide the inspiration and incentive for early years education and childcare practitioners to stop, look and take stock, she demonstrates how both the wood and the trees can be used to create magical thinking spaces that can't fail to be irresistible to children and adults alike!'

Kay Errington, Early Years Service Manager
Bournemouth Borough Council

A Place to Talk *in* Pre-schools

Elizabeth Jarman

Reprinted 2009 (twice)
Published 2009 by A&C Black Publishers Limited
36 Soho Square, London W1D 3QY
www.acblack.com

First published 2008 by Featherstone Education Limited

ISBN 978-1-9060-2925-8

Text © Elizabeth Jarman
Photographs © Elizabeth Jarman

A CIP record for this publication is available from the British Library.

Printed in Great Britain by Martins the Printer Berwick-upon-Tweed

This book is produced using paper that is made from wood grown in
managed, sustainable forests. It is natural, renewable and recyclable.
The logging and manufacturing processes conform to the environmental
regulations of the country of origin.

To see our full range of titles
visit www.acblack.com

Introduction

The recent I CAN report[1] suggests that over 50% of children in England are starting school with some form of speech and language difficulty or disability. The Early Years Foundation Stage reinforces that "the development and use of communication and language is at the heart of young children's learning."[2] Improving children's speaking and listening skills, has never been so important.

This resource considers the significant role that the physical environment can play in supporting children's speaking and listening skills; in supporting inquisitive, verbal experimentation, not just answering questions!

It includes a summary of some of the key environmental influences, collated from research studies; it includes lots of examples of what this looks like in practice; it poses questions to prompt action and it sign-posts you to further information.

We hope that this resource will challenge and inspire practitioners working in Pre-schools to create really effective 'places to talk'.

Developed alongside key Early Years developments, for example Every Child Matters, the Early Years Foundation Stage and Communicating Matters, 'A Place to Talk' has been recognised as an exciting and informative tool.

[1] *Cost to the Nation,* I CAN, 2006

[2] QCA/DfES: Curriculum Guidance for the Foundation Stage, p45

Contents

A Place to Talk *in* Pre-schools

Five environmental factors to consider

Following a review of research and practice in Early Years settings across England and Wales, we have identified five really important environmental points to consider when creating spaces designed to encourage children's speaking and listening skills.

1. *The physical environment should reflect the pedagogy[3] of the setting.*

Establishing a shared team understanding of your pedagogy will inform the way that you plan your learning environment. The way that a physical space is arranged says a lot to children about what is expected there and the sort of interactions welcome. It's really important that the learning environment and pedagogy connect and support one another.

2. *Practitioners should make the most of the space available, both inside and out.*

It's important to view learning spaces as a whole, including both inside and out and make the most of what's available. Across the space, children need secure spaces to talk where they feel comfortable and relaxed.

3. *Spaces should take account of physical factors that can impact on learning; for example, noise, colour and light.*

Noise

Being in a noisy environment makes it really difficult for children to concentrate. This can have a negative effect on their speaking and listening skills.

Colour

Colours need to be chosen carefully as they can affect children's behaviour and ability to focus and engage in conversation.

---

[3] *pedagogy* is your 'teaching' style

Light

Current research confirms that we are all energized by natural sunlight and that children learn faster in spaces with natural light. Light can be used to create mood and define an area.

4. The environment should not be over stimulating.

Too much choice can be overwhelming. Storage options should therefore be carefully considered.

The purpose and positioning of displays needs review. For example, it makes sense not to have a busy, cluttered display in an area where children are expected to focus say on a story book at group time.

5. Spaces should be viewed from the child's perspective.

Informed by a thorough understanding of how language develops we should keenly observe what the children are actually doing and how they are responding to the spaces we create, in order to plan appropriate, flexible environments that stimulate speaking and listening skills.

Twelve ideas to try

Inspired by practice from many settings, we have created twelve 'places to talk' that reflect the five environmental factors.

Each idea is spread over two pages:

➢ There is a 'starter' photograph of the space and a description of how we created it.

➢ We have included key points about why we chose those particular materials, why we positioned the furniture as we did and so on.

➢ There are also some photographs of children using the space, with their comments and some observations of what they did.

➢ We have included some action points for you to consider.

You'll see that what we are talking about does not have to cost a fortune, in fact you may already have some of the materials and resources that we have used. What it does involve though, is an informed view, keen observation skills which inform planning, so that you create the sort of environment that reflects what you want for children in your setting.

We acknowledge that opportunities for speaking and listening are everywhere, and we hope that these ideas will inspire you to review and develop some special 'places to talk' in your setting.

An interactive display space

How and why?

Children find it really difficult to relate to displays up high and yet many settings have display boards at adult eye level. Some have started to use these display boards to document children's learning, to share the process of learning with parents/carers, preferring to develop child height interactive displays for the children to explore, which of course stimulate language.

This is a simple display area set up to extend the children's interest in 'under the sea'. Keeping it uncluttered and thinking carefully about the presentation of the resources have made it an inviting space, offering a 'point of interest' in the setting.

A Place to Talk *in* Pre-schools

"These are all jangly," Chloe said about the shell mobile. This display appeals to lots of the senses. She explored the shells, stroking the smooth ones and then holding them to her ear, listening to for the sea. "It's always there," she said.

Offering interesting resources like this can help trigger all sorts of thought processes for children, helping them connect with past experiences. Chloe explored the shell textures and compared their colour tones.

This space was set up in a quiet area with little distracting flow of movement. This impacted on the way that the children were able to engage with the resources. Look at the concentration on Chloe's face.

Action

Review your displays. How do the children relate and interact with them? Who are they for? How could you make your displays more interactive and meaningful? Do they trigger talk?

A 'visually calm' space

How and why?

Children can find playing with playdough incredibly therapeutic and relaxing. Around the dough table is a great place to talk, or just to 'be'.

Here we have created a space offering carefully selected natural materials to stimulate talk and thinking along with the dough. Resources are clearly presented and there are not too many. We have avoided the temptation to over resource the area!

A Place to Talk *in* Pre-schools

This setting uses lots of neutral colours to keep the space calm and visually uncluttered.

Bold, bright colours can over stimulate children. Many settings find that colour is layered on through colourful cloths, aprons and equipment.

It's important therefore to consider the use of calming colours if you are creating a quiet space, as the environment impacts on children's dispositions and ability to focus.

Action

Look around your setting and consider the impact of an overload of contrasting colours on a child who is trying to concentrate. Do you have any visually calm areas? If not, create one and see what difference it makes to the children's behaviours and language.

A cosy space

How and why?

Children like to be in enclosed, cosy spaces. This space offers them a place to retreat, for a rest or a private chat with a friend. We used a pop up structure, a rug, soft toys, blankets and cushions in calming colours so that the space was relaxing.

The group decided that only four children could go inside the 'tent'. They also agreed that everyone had to take their shoes off. This was negotiated by a core group, who quickly took ownership of the space, establishing who could and couldn't come in and using their communication skills to enforce this!

Some of the children in the pre-school found the day very long and really enjoyed having a rest in the space. It was recognised as the children's favourite space in the setting and a place where staff observed high quality interaction between the children.

Action

Does your setting offer soft spaces or chill out areas? Where do children go to if they want a rest or a private chat? How could you create a space to support this?

A space for one

How and why?

It's really important to view the environment from the child's perspective; how it looks, sounds and feels, so that we can create spaces to support children appropriately.

In a busy, often hectic environment, children need spaces to withdraw to, so that they can reflect, process their thinking and language and generally make sense of what is going on around them. This swing offers an ideal enclosed space for one.

A Place to Talk *in* Pre-schools

This space offered Chloe a secure spot. At this pre-school, it was important to plan spaces like this as timid children in particular were finding the energetic group of children attending the setting too noisy at times.

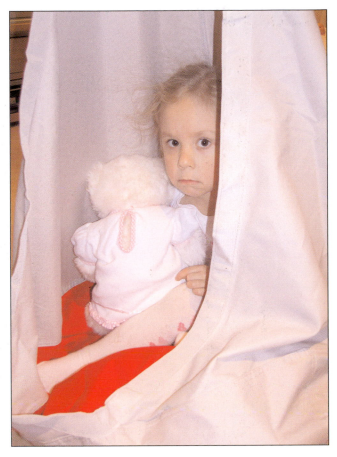

The swing provided a space where Chloe could observe and see what the other children were doing while having some quiet time alone.

Action

Do you have any small spaces where children can reflect, watch and think? Create some and notice who uses them. Is the quality of the language different in a small space?

A pleasant space

How and why?

The sink area provides a natural meeting place where lots of conversation goes on! We enhanced this space with some framed pictures of tropical fish, building on a child's interest from home. We added some bamboo, because of its unusual appearance and also some pot pourri, as understandably some children are put off using the bathrooms when they smell! We also changed the big industrial looking bin with a flip lid, which some children were frightened of and used an open low level bin between the sinks.

"My dad's got these in his garden" said Thomas.

Carefully chosen and positioned points of interest around a setting can stimulate lots of talk especially when they help children make connections with past experiences or home.

Action

Have a look at your bathroom spaces. Could you enhance them? How could you capitalise on the natural conversations that go on there? Where could you add 'points of interest' in your setting?

A space to support selection

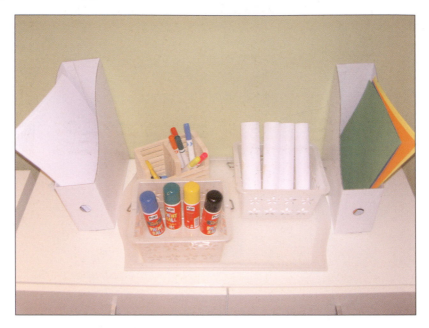

How and why?

Resources set out in a clear, uncluttered way support children's planning and decision making skills, helping them to make choices about how they want to represent their ideas.

Using neutral, uniform containers stops the 'riot of colour' often seen in settings. Too much bold bright primary colour can be visually over stimulating for children, making it difficult for them to concentrate. Here, a selection of resources are available at child height and offered in a manageable way to encourage independence.

Ruby talks to Julie (see opposite) about what's on offer and what she might do. The basket allows Ruby to collect what she wants to use. Julie supports but allows Ruby to make choices independently. The activity is open ended.

Ruby then spent an hour, deeply engaged in cutting, sticking and selecting more materials as needed. Ruby chose to work on the floor.

Julie observed from a distance, recording Ruby's behaviour and communication skills, verbal and non-verbal. She also observed how Ruby was interacting with the resources in the space and how the area was supporting her independence, selection and thinking skills, all essential for good communication.

Action

How can you offer resources to allow independent choice? Do you have too much on offer? Try setting up a small space like the one in the photo, with carefully selected storage containers and materials. How does this impact on the way that children use the materials?

A space for digging

How and why?

Outside spaces offer a rich opportunity for talk. There's so much to observe, so much to notice. This pre-school used railway sleepers to contain lots of soil for digging. In wet weather, the soil became really interesting and muddy, offering a wonderful stimulus for conversation.

Henry spent most of the session hard at work with a group of friends.

They dug a hole together. It was hard work.

"That's our hole. I've got to put more mud in it," he said.

The group kept standing in the hole to see if the mud covered their wellies! Lots of descriptive language was triggered and the group were completely absorbed in the activity for a sustained period.

Action

Do you make the most of language opportunities in your outside space? An area like this one is easy to arrange and offers ongoing interest, as the soil texture changes according to the weather. Try setting up an area like this and record the sort of talk that goes on. Who uses the space? How long do they spend there? How will this inform your future provision?

A Place to Talk *in* Pre-schools

An enclosed, child height space

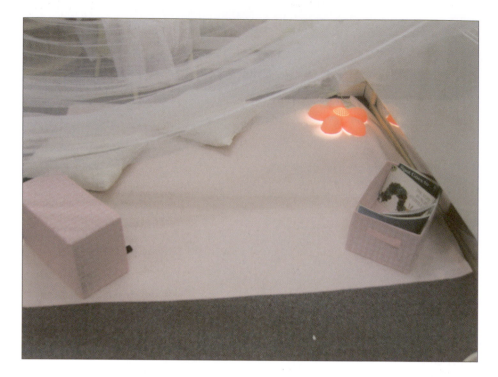

How and why?

This setting has really high ceilings. When staff looked at the ceiling from child height, they felt it looked like a warehouse.

We lowered the ceiling in this area by using a drape, creating a really intimate and inviting space for the children to crawl into.

We added a lamp and fluffy soft blanket to define the space, making it comfortable. We added simple storage boxes containing finger puppets and a selection of books. We deliberately kept it simple and clutter free.

A Place to Talk *in* Pre-schools

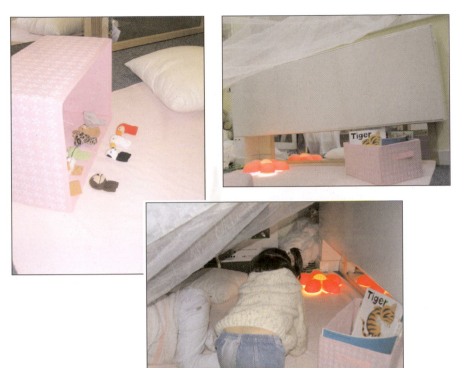

The children really liked the cosiness of the space. Adults were too big to get in. It was the children's space. There was little verbal but lots of non-verbal communication. The children explored the resources on offer and enjoyed just being in there.

Action

How could you lower your ceilings and use lighting to create mood and atmosphere?

A 'snack time' space

How and why?

Snack time offers a wonderful opportunity for informal talk. This setting offered ongoing snack provision so that children could have their snack when it fitted in with their schedule during the session.

The space was in a quiet part of the setting. A selection of interesting fruit was on offer to stimulate conversation. The space was in a very colourful room so we calmed it down by adding a neutral table cloth and drape on the wall next to the table. The space was set up to encourage independence and four places were arranged so that children could choose what they wanted to eat and prepare it themselves.

A Place to Talk *in* Pre-schools

"These seeds will grow into beanstalks," explained Tiger-Lily.

"I prefer bananas," said William.

Lisa supported the children but let them make choices and explore the fruit on offer. Being with such a small group gave her a wonderful opportunity to listen to the talk that went on. She was careful not to ask too many questions and direct the conversation but to observe and listen to what the children had to say.

Action

How could you re-work your snack time to fit in with the children's needs and capitalise on this natural, informal opportunity for talk?

A multi-purpose space

How and why?

We made use of the many tables in this setting, using the space they offered underneath. We used a long piece of net curtaining and a blanket to enclose the space and a textured bathmat to add interest. We added some cushions, a light to add atmosphere and some simple story props.

A Place to Talk *in* Pre-schools

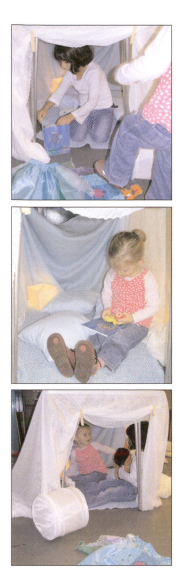

Aisha and Isabella explored the space.

"It's an under the sea tent," said Isabella. *"We could play mermaids. The light is on."*

"These are cushions. They could be the sea if you like that?" Aisha said.

Complex language and planning of the game followed. The two girls were focused and used the space to explore the finger puppets, to dress up, read the book and then developed their game which moved away from the under the sea idea completely. They used the space as a base for their play. It was a multipurpose area, but one which offered them enclosure and privacy, to which they responded well.

Action

Does your environment support child led play to develop? Children's language will be much more engaged when they are involved in self-initiated play.

A themed space

How and why?

This space was created using an unfolded cardboard box which was made into the front of a house, offering an entrance. It was supported by two tables. The draped ceiling enclosed the space, offering a private story space.

A Place to Talk *in* Pre-schools

Inside Pooh's House, we displayed a collection of books about Pooh Bear and some soft character toys. The children however, decided it was a castle and then a submarine. Although some played with the story props available, much of the activity involved exploring the space which offered different places to sit and read and under table spaces to lie down with a book. The children sought out spaces which allowed them to spread out reinforcing the need for children to have spaces without tables and chairs.

> **Action**
>
> How could you create a multipurpose space like this one, which could set the scene for lots of imaginative language activity?

A space for choices

How and why?

Making everything available to children all of the time can make for an overly busy, hectic environment. Too much choice can overwhelm children. It can also make it difficult for children to manage the resources when it's time to tidy up.

It's obviously important that children have access to a range of materials and resources throughout the week, so this pre-school created a 'choices area'. Photos of children using various activities were available to review in a photo album and on the 'choices tree'. This triggered lots of discussion between children and staff, allowing children to help plan what they wanted to access in the next session.

"The children really like this area because it gives them the chance to talk about things they've done before. They love it when the things they choose are there when they come in the next day. We tend to do this in one or two spaces in the pre-school and it helps us keep the environment less cluttered. We still have lots of core equipment out all the time. Talk in the choices area is really purposeful and it gives us a chance to hear about what things the children really like. It's helpful for our observations."

Julie, staff member.

"What do you want to do? Look at this game. I'm going to play with it. Chloe likes it," she explained to the teddy.

Staff found that adding soft toys to areas set up to support talk 'softened' the behaviour of children and encouraged calmer more relaxed dispositions.

Action

What systems do you have or could you set up to offer real choice to the children, so that they can manage materials and resources independently?

Action points

Here is a summary of the questions we posed to prompt action. Use them to reflect on the environment that you currently provide for children and then to help you focus on making positive changes.

➢ Review your displays. How do the children relate and interact with them? Who are they for? How could you make your displays more interactive and meaningful? Do they trigger talk?

➢ Look around your setting and consider the impact of an overload of contrasting colours on a child who is trying to concentrate. Do you have any visually calm areas? If not, create one and see what difference it makes to the children's behaviours and language.

➢ Does your setting offer soft spaces or chill out areas? Where do children go to if they want a rest or a private chat? How could you create a space to support this?

➢ Do you have any small spaces where children can reflect, watch and think? Create some and notice who uses them. Is the quality of the language different in a small space?

➢ Have a look at your bathroom spaces. Could you enhance them? How could you capitalise on the natural conversations that go on there? Where could you add 'points of interest' in your setting?

➢ How can you offer resources to allow independent choice? Do you have too much on offer? How does this impact on the way that children use the materials?

➢ Do you make the most of language opportunities in your outside space?

➢ How could you lower your ceilings and use lighting to create mood and atmosphere?

➢ How could you re-work your snack time to fit in with the children's needs and capitalise on this natural informal opportunity for talk?

> Does your environment support child led activity? Children's language will be much more engaged when they are involved in self-initiated play.

> How could you create a multipurpose space, which could set the scene for lots of imaginative language activity?

> What's your role in supporting children's speaking and listening skills?

Useful resources

The resources that we used to create our 'places to talk' were easy to source and inexpensive. They included:

> Net curtains

> Blankets in natural, relaxing colours

> Textured cushions

> Different sized rugs

> Interesting objects to stimulate talk, e.g. smooth stones, pine cones, corks and shells

> Drapes to enclose spaces

> Lamps to define spaces

> Cardboard boxes

> Pegs

Further references and useful websites

The Communication Friendly Spaces Toolkit: Improving Speaking and Listening Skills in the Early Years Foundation Stage. Jarman, Elizabeth (2007). ISBN: 1-859-90428-9. Can be ordered from Prolog (0870 600 2400)

Cost to the Nation, I CAN, 2006, available from www.ican.org.uk

www.pge.com for information about studies on the way day lighting affects children's learning

Policy for Effective Learning in the Foundation Stage. Jaeckle, S (2002) Bristol City Council Education Department

www.sightlines-initiative.com for information about the Reggio Emilia Children's Network, conferences and resources

www.quietclassrooms.org for guidance on controlling noise in settings and public places

www.colourtest.ue-foundation.org for information on the effects of colours on behaviour

Building for Sure Start: A design guide - integrated provision for under-fives. DfES, 2004. ISBN: 1-844-78196-8

Children, Spaces, Relations: Meta project for an environment for young children, Ceppi, G; Zini, M. (1998) Reggio Children Publications. ISBN: 8-887-96011-9

Other books in this series

A Place to Talk *in* Children's Centres

978 1 906029 27 X

A Place to Talk *in* Extended Schools

978 1 906029 28 8

A Place to Talk *in* Pack-away Settings

978 1 906029 26 1

all by Elizabeth Jarman

Thanks to all of the settings and practitioners who informed and inspired this publication, especially:

Newbold Children's Centre, Rochdale

Beaufort Community Centre, Bournemouth

Smarden Pre-School, Kent